BOX OF CIGAR BANDS

James C. McComb Sinclair II

Schiffer Publishing Ltd®

4880 Lower Valley Road • Atglen, PA 19310

Library of Congress Control Number: 2015947963

Designed by Justin Watkinson
Type set in Copperplate Gothic Std/Minion Pro

ISBN: 978-0-7643-4987-4
Printed in China

Published by Schiffer Publishing, Ltd.
4880 Lower Valley Road
Atglen, PA 19310
Phone: (610) 593-1777; Fax: (610) 593-2002
E-mail: Info@schifferbooks.com

For our complete selection of fine books on this and related subjects, please visit our website at www.schifferbooks.com. You may also write for a free catalog.

This book may be purchased from the publisher. Please try your bookstore first.

We are always looking for people to write books on new and related subjects. If you have an idea for a book, please contact us at proposals@schifferbooks.com.

Schiffer Publishing's titles are available at special discounts for bulk purchases for sales promotions or premiums. Special editions, including personalized covers, corporate imprints, and excerpts can be created in large quantities for special needs. For more information, contact the publisher.

I would like
to dedicate this
book to my late brother
Frederick Klair Sinclair Jr.

THE
STORY
OF THE
COLLECTION

Somewhere around the late 1950s, when I was a very young lad living in southeastern Pennsylvania, I remember my Uncle Leiper coming to our house for a visit. Uncle Leiper—whose full name was Thomas Leiper Black—was from an old prominent Philadelphia family and was a world traveler, along with my Aunt Virginia, who was my mother's oldest sister. I was always excited when Uncle Leiper and Aunt Virginia came to visit because they always brought presents. Not just any presents, but things that most young boys of that time would never get as a gift. They brought exciting things from all around the world. I remember finding a seat in the corner of our living room and waiting for the formalities of greeting my parents and my other brothers. I really don't recall what, if any, gift was given to me, but what was burned and forever ingrained into my mind was the gift that Uncle Leiper gave to my brother Klair. He received this collection of cigar bands preserved in a ledger book. The cigar bands were all displayed in neatly spaced rows that even at a young age I could tell was something special. There were pages upon pages of brightly colored bands with pictures of kings and queens, military figures, American presidents, and so much more. For several years, I tried to persuade my brother to trade something I owned, or a Christmas present or even money, but Klair always said no. Years passed and at one point I found myself helping him move into a new apartment. While unpacking a box I ran across the cigar band book. I held it up and started to try to bargain with him, but still to no avail. Years passed. About two years before my brother Frederick Klair Sinclair Jr. passed away, he stopped by the farm where my wife Ann and I live. He was carrying a paper bag when he walked in and said "you might as well have this" and handed it to me. To my delight, the bag contained the cigar band book that I had admired for over fifty years. He said "I am getting rid of my books because they collect too much dust and it bothers my allergies." This was a fabulous gift from my brother and I thanked him profusely for his kindness. A short time ago, after finishing a two volume compendium on World War Russian uniforms, I mentioned to my publisher that I had this collection of cigar bands and I thought it could be developed into an interesting book. Later I showed the collection to them and we agreed to proceed with the project. When I started to really get into the pages of the book and began looking at each cigar band through an optical magnifier, I saw an art form that I had not imagined. The ledger contained over a thousand examples of beautiful lithography from the golden age of cigar band production. I was able to do some research and found that the person whose name was in the book, Hugh Augustus Wilson, was born in Philadelphia October 1, 1888. I also found that there was a connection between the Leiper and Wilson family that dated back to the American Revolution. I do not know how the collection came into the possession of Thomas Leiper Black. This information, along with the time period of the collection, leads me to believe that Wilson, like so many other boys of his time, started collecting cigar bands as an inexpensive hobby and pastime. I have decided to display in this book the entire collection exactly as Master Wilson did in his original ledger book. Because of the used condition of many of the bands I believe the boy must have found them on the streets, on trolleys or trains, in hotel lobbies, and wherever he could. I have scanned them exactly as I have found them. There are so many beautifully detailed examples that I decided to enlarge some of the most beautiful bands and put them at the back of the book. Take a look at some of these enlarged portraits. Cigar manufacturers often hired very skilled and sometimes renowned artists as designers. These images are certainly a reflection of their talent.

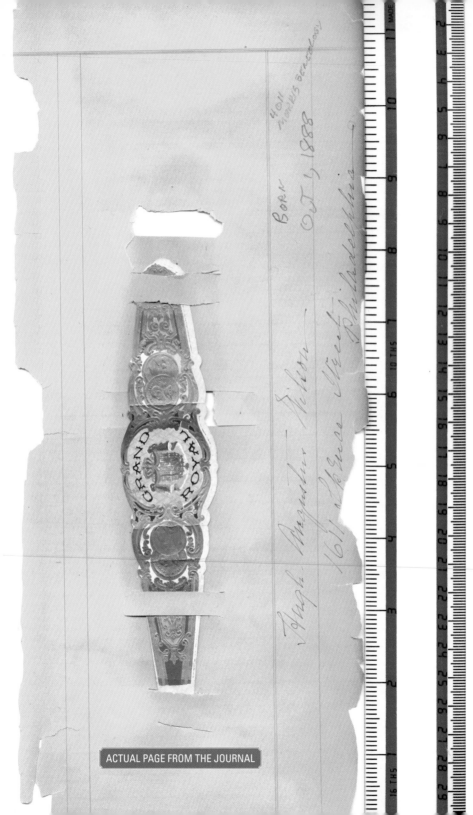

GRAND ROYAL

Joseph Augustus Wilson — Silver —
1611 Mervine Street Philadelphia

Born
Oct 4, 1888

401
Morris Street [crossed out]

A
BRIEF HISTORY
OF
CIGAR BANDS

There are several stories about why cigar bands were used and how they came to be. One tale is that the Russian Tsaritsa Catherine the Great wrapped her cigars in silk so as not to stain her fingers. Another story is that English gentlemen who wore white gloves as a fashion accessory in the early part of the nineteenth century put paper bands around their cigars so they would not leave tobacco stains. Who knows for sure? What is common knowledge is that sometime around 1830, a Dutchman by the name of Gustave Bock put a paper band around each cigar and wrote his signature on each band. There was a problem in the 1830s with people shipping cigars to overseas clients, claiming they were getting cigars from Cuba, when in fact they were not getting the better Cuban cigars. Cigar bands helped manufacturers label their product and also market their brand with advertising. The use of the cigar band became widespread almost immediately. At about the same time, lithography printing developed and matured into an industry of its own. Lithography comes from the Greek word for "writing with stone." The basis of this process was discovered by Aloysius Senefelder, who worked in Munich,

Germany, around 1796. This printing process really blossomed in the latter part of the nineteenth century. The cigar industry started using this new type of printing and the "Golden Age" of cigar art was born. During the late nineteenth and early twentieth centuries, the cigar industry embellished their product with elaborate designs, including portraits of famous people of the time, historical figures, mythological animals, and whatever else caught the imagination of the many artists who worked for cigar manufacturers. Company logos, commemorative events, and personalization became the industry standard for this ever increasing market. I have read that it is estimated that at the turn of the twentieth century, eighty percent of American men smoked cigars and about two billion cigar bands were made each year. Cigar bands are a colorful piece of history; it is no wonder they were collected by so many adolescent boys. I am sure that young Hugh Augustus Wilson was fascinated and inspired while spending hours collecting and carefully mounting his collection in his ledger book. I hope that you will find the bands as exciting and interesting to look at as he did.

THE
CIGAR BANDS

SHOWN IN ACTUAL SIZE

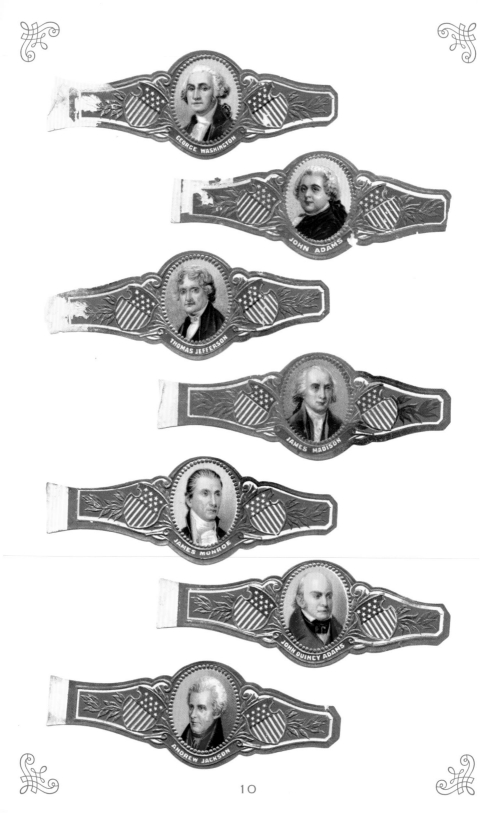

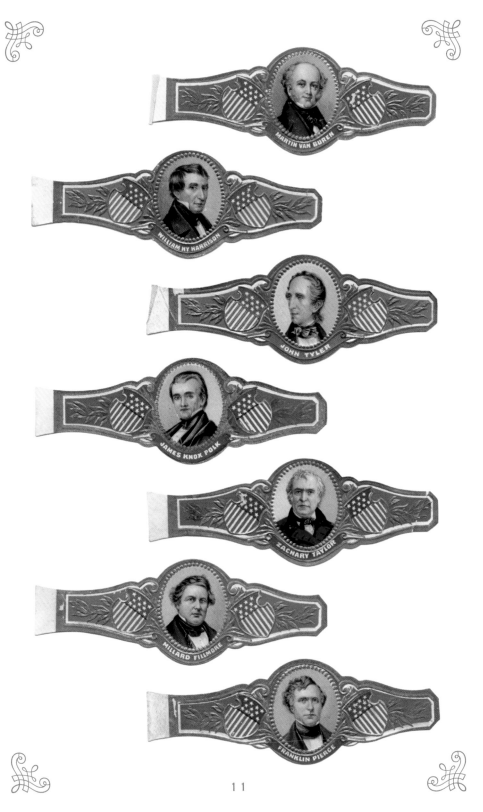

MARTIN VAN BUREN

WILLIAM HY HARRISON

JOHN TYLER

JAMES KNOX POLK

ZACHARY TAYLOR

MILLARD FILLMORE

FRANKLIN PIERCE

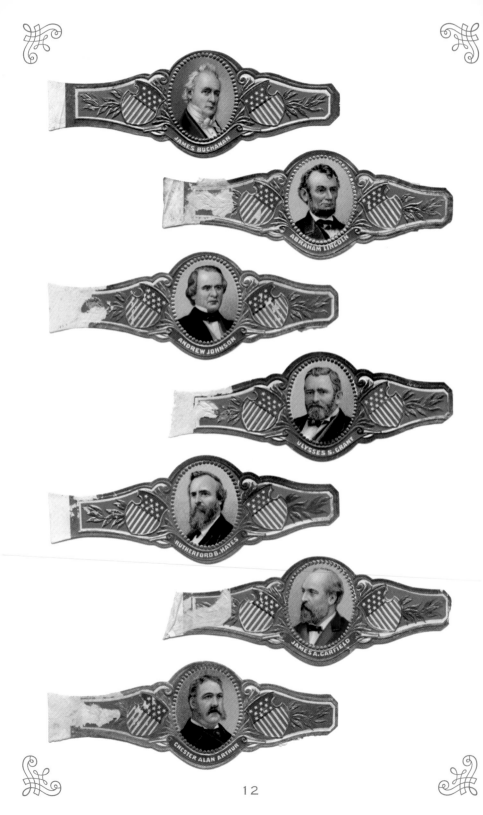

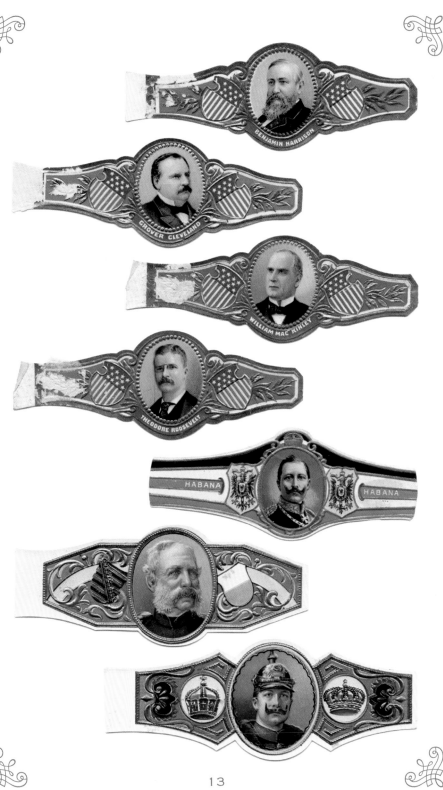

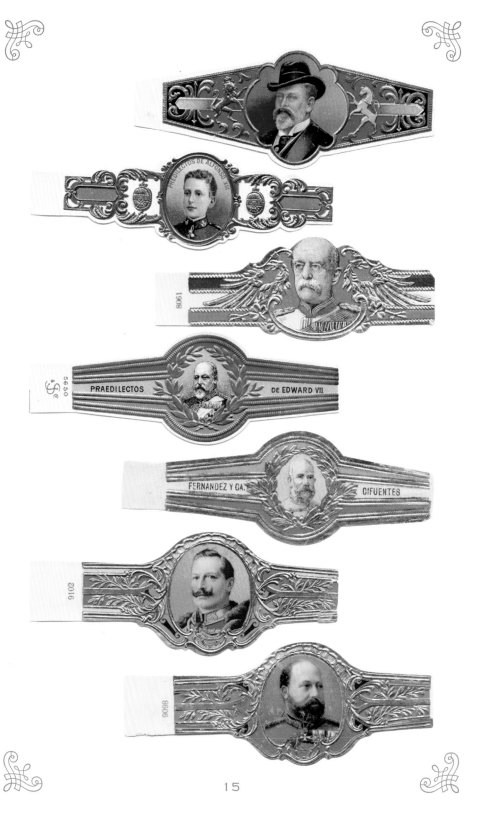

PREDILECTOS DE ALFONSO XIII

8061

PRAEDILECTOS 5650 DE EDWARD VII

FERNANDEZ Y CA. CIFUENTES

2016

8608

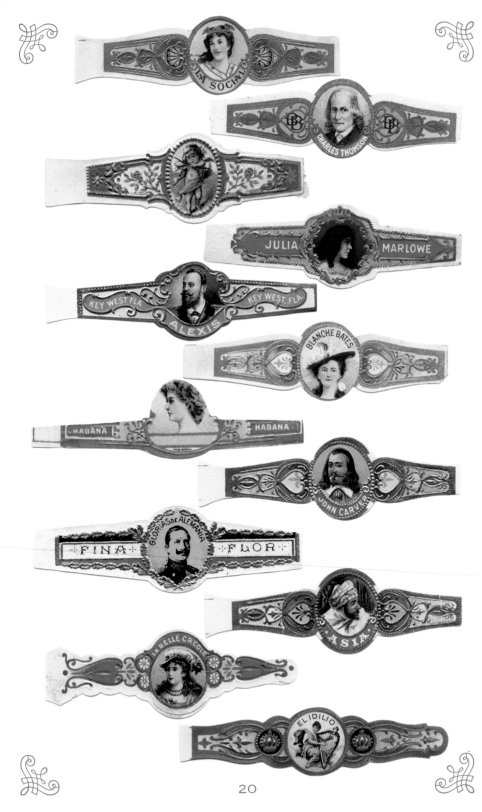

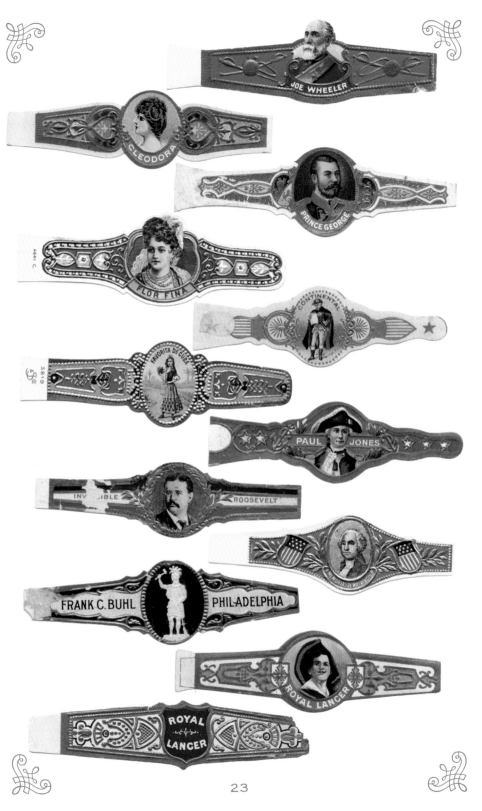

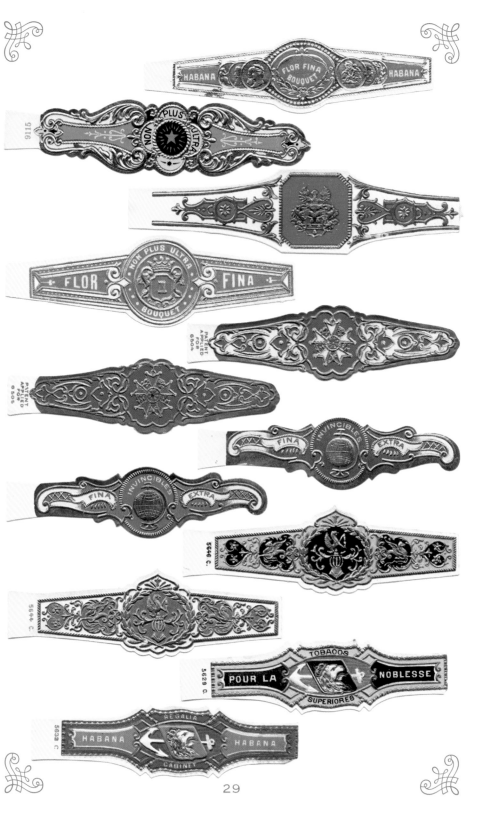

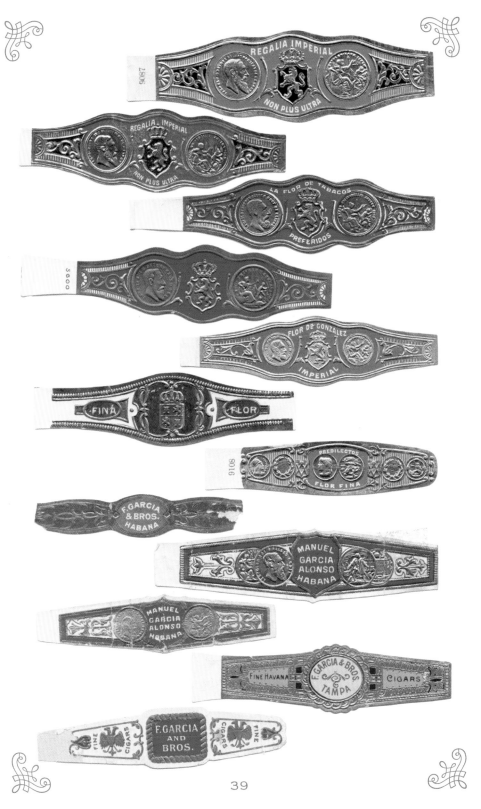

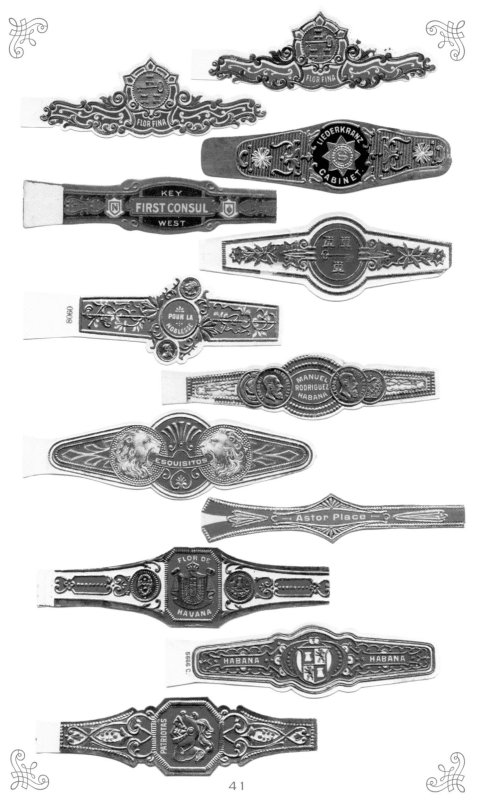

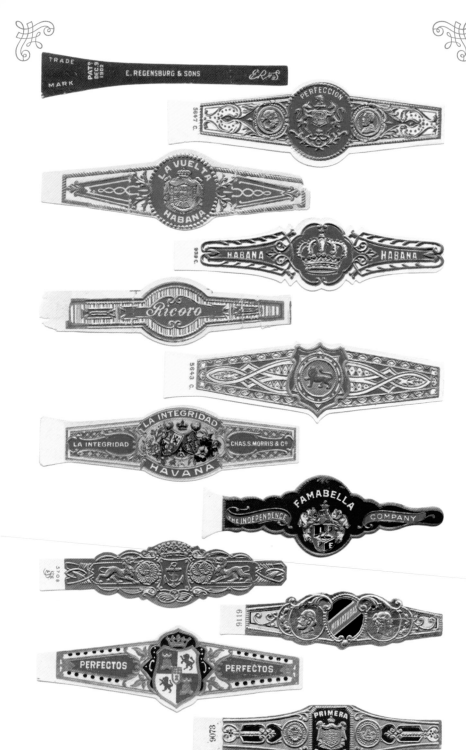

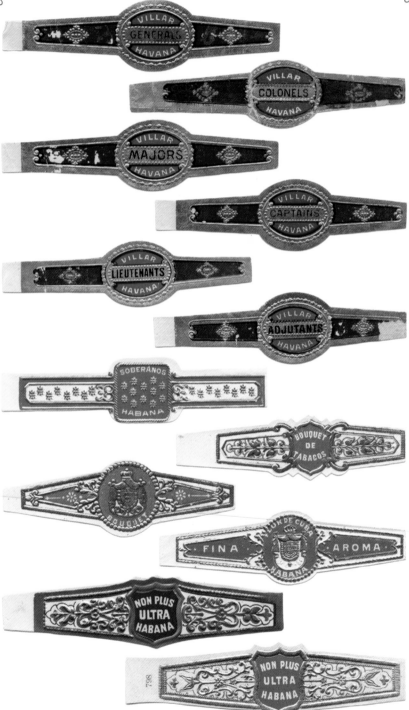

O. H.
NETHERWOOD   HABANA   NETHERWOOD

ALL HAVANA FILLER CUBANOLA 5¢ CIGAR — ALL HAVANA FILLER CUBANOLA 5¢ CIGAR — ALL HAVANA FILLER CUBANOLA 5¢ CIGAR — ALL HAVANA FILLER CUBANOLA 5¢

CREMO   CREMO   CREMO   CREMO

PRINCESAS

ROSA ROMA

MINISTROS

FLOR   FINA

"How is Your Wiring"
see
SCHOENBERG

PERFECTO

FONSECA

Bellevue B·S Stratford

REGALIA SALON

FLOR ESCEPCIONALES FINA

TABACOS HABANOS

FLOR FINA

FLOR FINA

NON PLUS ULTRA FLOR FINA

UNION LEAGUE CIGAR

BOUQUET REINA FINA

BOUQUET

TOBACOS SUPERIORES

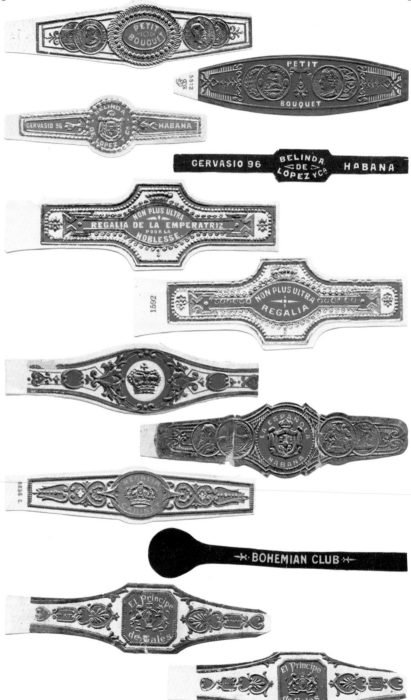

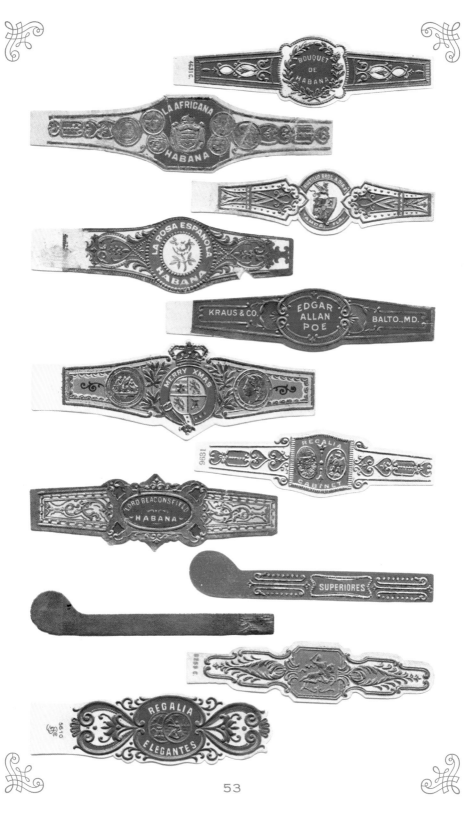

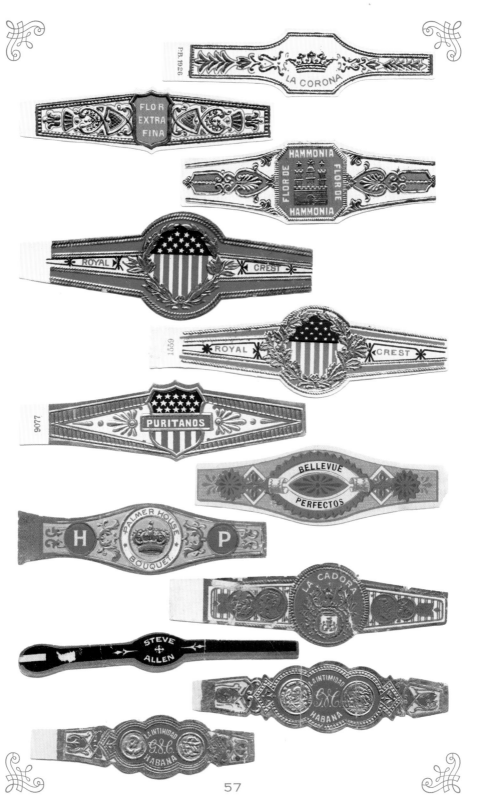

REGALIA BOUQUET

EL INVIGRO — CLEAR HAVANA — CLEAR HAVANA

LE TRIOMPHE — HABANA

TABACOS ESQUISITOS — LA HILDA — CIGAR FAC'Y

HABANA CABINETS

HABANA SUPERFINOS

Art — ALL HAVANA — ALL HAVANA

INVINCIBLES — HABANA

POUR LA — NOBLESSE

CONCHAS — EXTRAS

BOUQUET — DE HABANA

JULES VERNE — HABANA — HABANA

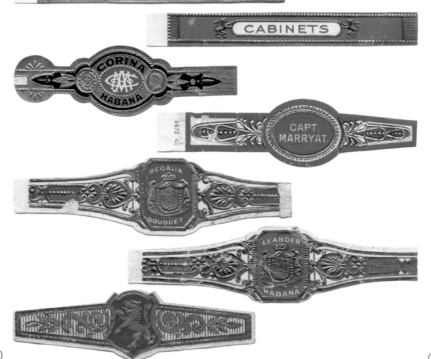

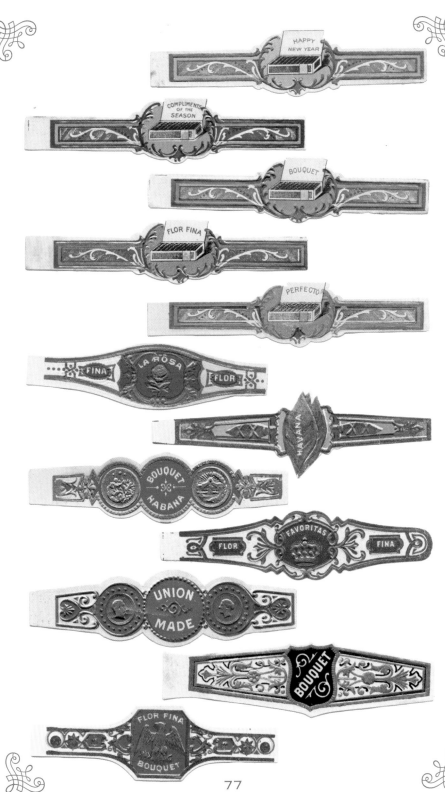

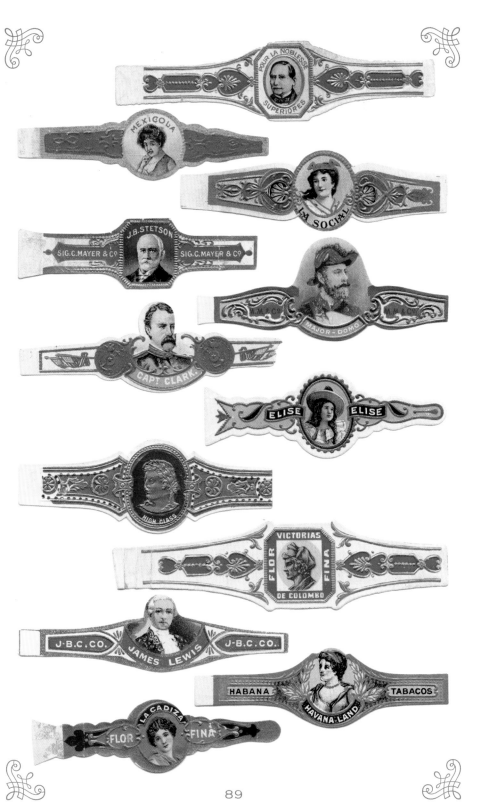

DETAILED
VIEWS

SEE PAGE 10

SEE PAGE 10

SEE PAGE 10

SEE PAGE 10

SEE PAGE 10

SEE PAGE 10

ANDREW JACKSON

SEE PAGE 10

MARTIN VAN BUREN

SEE PAGE 11

WILLIAM HY HARRISON

SEE PAGE 11

JOHN TYLER

SEE PAGE 11

SEE PAGE 11

SEE PAGE 11

SEE PAGE 11

SEE PAGE 11

SEE PAGE 12

SEE PAGE 12

SEE PAGE 12

SEE PAGE 12

SEE PAGE 12

SEE PAGE 12

SEE PAGE 12

SEE PAGE 13

SEE PAGE 13

SEE PAGE 13

SEE PAGE 13

SEE PAGE 13

SEE PAGE 13

SEE PAGE 13

SEE PAGE 14

SEE PAGE 14

SEE PAGE 14

SEE PAGE 14

SEE PAGE 14

SEE PAGE 15

SEE PAGE 14

SEE PAGE 15

SEE PAGE 15

SEE PAGE 15

PRAEDILECTOS · DE EDWARD VII · 5650

SEE PAGE 15

FERNANDEZ Y CA. · CIFUENTES

SEE PAGE 15

2016

SEE PAGE 15

8608

SEE PAGE 15

SEE PAGE 16

DE ALEMANA · GLORIAS

SEE PAGE 16

SEE PAGE 16

SEE PAGE 16

SEE PAGE 16

SEE PAGE 16

SEE PAGE 17

SEE PAGE 17

SEE PAGE 18

SEE PAGE 18

SEE PAGE 19

SEE PAGE 19

SEE PAGE 19

SEE PAGE 19

SEE PAGE 19

SEE PAGE 19

SEE PAGE 19

SEE PAGE 19

SEE PAGE 19

SEE PAGE 19

SEE PAGE 20

SEE PAGE 20

SEE PAGE 20

SEE PAGE 20

SEE PAGE 20

SEE PAGE 20

SEE PAGE 20

SEE PAGE 20

SEE PAGE 20

SEE PAGE 20

SEE PAGE 20

SEE PAGE 21

SEE PAGE 21

SEE PAGE 21

SEE PAGE 21

SEE PAGE 21

SEE PAGE 21

SEE PAGE 21

SEE PAGE 21

HABANA · HABANA

SEE PAGE 21

· FINA · · GLORIAS DE MADRID · · FLOR ·

12491

SEE PAGE 21

LA NATALIA

SEE PAGE 22

Havana Cigars.

JOHN HAY

SEE PAGE 22

SEE PAGE 22

SEE PAGE 22

SEE PAGE 22

SEE PAGE 22

SEE PAGE 22

SEE PAGE 22

SEE PAGE 22

SEE PAGE 22

SEE PAGE 22

SEE PAGE 22

SEE PAGE 23

SEE PAGE 23

SEE PAGE 23

SEE PAGE 23

SEE PAGE 23

SEE PAGE 23

SEE PAGE 23

SEE PAGE 23

SEE PAGE 23

SEE PAGE 23

SEE PAGE 23

SEE PAGE 24

SEE PAGE 24

SEE PAGE 24

SEE PAGE 24

SEE PAGE 24

SEE PAGE 28

SEE PAGE 31

SEE PAGE 32

SEE PAGE 36

SEE PAGE 37

SEE PAGE 39

SEE PAGE 41

SEE PAGE 42

SEE PAGE 43

SEE PAGE 45

SEE PAGE 47

SEE PAGE 48

SEE PAGE 53

SEE PAGE 56

SEE PAGE 58

SEE PAGE 61

SEE PAGE 62

SEE PAGE 63

SEE PAGE 63

SEE PAGE 63

SEE PAGE 63

SEE PAGE 64

FINA **9108** FLOR

SEE PAGE 66

VICTORIA **12488** VICTORIA

VICTORIA

SEE PAGE 66

HENRY THE FOURTH

BUSTILLO BROS. & DIAZ

SEE PAGE 66

Y.O.M.C.

MANUEL CHAVEZ Y CA. YBOR CITY TAMPA FLA.

SEE PAGE 66

ESPECIALES

SEE PAGE 66

LA SOLVENCIA

HIGH   GRADE

SEE PAGE 66

LA HILDA

CLEAR   HAVANA

PHILADELPHIA

SEE PAGE 66

LA TOCO

LA TOCO   T & O. Cº

SEE PAGE 66

SEE PAGE 66

SEE PAGE 66

SEE PAGE 66

SEE PAGE 67

12588

SEE PAGE 67

96096

SEE PAGE 68

9060

EXTRAFINOS

GLORIAS DE EDUARDO VII

IMPERIALES

SEE PAGE 68

9061

IMPERIAL

REINA ALEJANDRA

BRITANICA

SEE PAGE 69

SEE PAGE 73

SEE PAGE 73

SEE PAGE 74

SEE PAGE 74

SEE PAGE 75

SEE PAGE 76

SEE PAGE 78

SEE PAGE 78

SEE PAGE 79

SEE PAGE 79

SEE PAGE 79

SEE PAGE 79

SEE PAGE 82

SEE PAGE 83

SEE PAGE 83

SEE PAGE 84

SEE PAGE 85

SEE PAGE 85

SEE PAGE 86

SEE PAGE 87

SEE PAGE 89

SEE PAGE 89

SEE PAGE 89

SEE PAGE 89

SEE PAGE 89

SEE PAGE 89

SEE PAGE 89

SEE PAGE 89

SEE PAGE 89

SEE PAGE 91

SEE PAGE 91

SEE PAGE 91

SEE PAGE 91

SEE PAGE 93

SEE PAGE 93

SEE PAGE 93

SEE PAGE 93

SEE PAGE 94

SEE PAGE 94

SEE PAGE 95

SEE PAGE 95

SEE PAGE 95

SEE PAGE 95

SEE PAGE 95